Welcome

Written by Michael L. Morgan
Illustrations by Patrick Prince

Welcome
Copyright © 2020 by Michael L. Morgan

All rights reserved. No part of this publication may be reproduced, distributed, or transmitted in any form or by any means, including photocopying, recording, or other electronic or mechanical methods, without the prior written permission of the author, except in the case of brief quotations embodied in critical reviews and certain other non-commercial uses permitted by copyright law.

Tellwell Talent
www.tellwell.ca

ISBN
978-0-2288-3697-1 (Hardcover)
978-0-2288-3696-4 (Paperback)

Welcome
Welcome
And welcome again

It's good to have you here,
in Toronto my friend

Home of the Blue Jays and TFC,
the Raptors the Argos, and our beloved Leafs

In Patriot love, we welcome you all,
the dark, the light, the great, the small

There's so much to see, and plenty to do,
No matter the season, it's all here for you

Visit the Capybara's magicians they are, escaped for a few days from the High Park farm

There's much to be 'CN', you'll feel you can fly,
as you circle the Tower, way up in the sky

Come experience the arts, seasoned with zest, come and learn from our schools, they're simply the best

Our parks are neat, and you'll love our theaters
Our zoo's pretty good and our mayor's not bad either

We have lots of street fests and a hand full of parades, and when you feel tired, on TORONTO, you'll laze

All this awaits you when you come to say hi, and if you're only here for a visit, we'll sadly say bye

Thank you for coming,
and please tell a friend

Welcome
Welcome
And Welcome again

www.ingramcontent.com/pod-product-compliance
Lightning Source LLC
LaVergne TN
LVHW072017060526
838200LV00059B/4691